# ISAAC JOHNSON
## From Slave to Stonecutter

# ISAAC JOHNSON
## From Slave to Stonecutter

Hope Irvin Marston

*Illustrated by Maria Magdalena Brown*

COBBLEHILL BOOKS     Dutton   New York

Library of Congress Cataloging-in-Publication Data
Marston, Hope Irvin.
Isaac Johnson : from slave to stonecutter / Hope Irvin Marston :
illustrated by Maria Magdalena Brown.
p.    cm.
Includes bibliographical references and index.
ISBN 0-525-65165-9
1. Johnson, Isaac, 1844–1905—Juvenile literature. 2. Fugitive
slaves—Kentucky—Biography—Juvenile literature. 3. Slaves—United
States—Social conditions—Juvenile literature. I. Brown, Maria
Magdalena. II. Title.
E450.J684M37    1995    976.9'041'092—dc20    [B]    94-32671    CIP    AC

Published in the United States by Cobblehill Books,
an affiliate of Dutton Children's Books,
a division of Penguin Books USA Inc.
375 Hudson Street, New York, New York 10014

Designed by Jean Krulis

Printed in the United States of America
First Edition 10 9 8 7 6 5 4 3 2 1

*To Pauline Tedford and E. Jane Layo*

Thanks for keeping the memory
of Isaac Johnson alive in Waddington.

# Acknowledgments

*I am grateful to the following people for their help in my research of Isaac Johnson:*

To Shirley Tramontona, Stu Wilson, and Tom Price of the St. Lawrence County Historical Museum, who introduced me to Isaac Johnson;

To Pauline Tedford, Deputy Historian, and E. Jane Layo, Waddington Town Historian, who chauffeured me to the places where Isaac lived and worked on both sides of the St. Lawrence River;

To Fran LaFlamme, Clarence Cross, Jack Schecter, and Lynne O'Brien Cook for help in researching Isaac's life in Upper Canada;

To Rev. Gilbert Menard, Pastor, Immaculate Heart of Mary Church, Churubusco, NY, and Evelyn Watson, Town Clerk of Churubusco;

To Persis Boyesen, Ogdensburg Historian, and Sister Mary Christine Taylor, Academic Dean, Wadams Hall, Ogdensburg, NY;

To Dr. Cornel Reinhart, Assistant Professor of History, St. Lawrence University;

To Michael O. Smith, University of Michigan, for information on black regiments in Michigan;

To Hattie Clements, Pat Craven, and Margaret J. Schroeder, my able researchers in Bardstown, KY; to Carolyn Murray-Wooley, author of *Rock Fences of the Bluegrass*; to James M. Prichard, Archivist, Kentucky Department of Libraries and Archives; and to The Filson Club, Louisville, KY;

To Father Jerry E. Nadine, grandson of Isaac Johnson, for his encouragement throughout my research;

To the staff at the Post Library, Fort Drum, NY, for allowing me to borrow whatever I needed for my research;

To Sandy Lamb, Librarian, Black River Free Library, for securing me an abundance of research materials through Interlibrary Loan.

# CONTENTS

# Author's Note

THIS BIOGRAPHY OF ISAAC JOHNSON is based on his own book, *Slavery Days in Old Kentucky*, which he wrote in 1901. Isaac Johnson was born a slave and experienced the hardships and cruelties of slavery. He wrote his book in order to let readers know what slavery was like, and how the system had no merit for either whites or blacks. He described his actual experience as a slave, so that others would understand what slavery meant and would never let the same thing happen again.

His forty-page booklet was published privately in Ogdensburg, New York, in 1904. It was not widely distributed. Copies were recently discovered in the archives of the St. Lawrence County Historical Society, the Special Collections of the Ogdensburg Public Library, the Owen D. Young Library archives at St. Lawrence University, and the library of Eastern Kentucky University.

His story ends with the Civil War, and to complete it I have researched the areas where Isaac Johnson lived after the war, from Kentucky to Michigan to the St. Lawrence Valley. I learned a lot about his life after the war through Isaac's pension records and in talking with two of his descendants. I obtained anecdotes from individuals whose fathers and grandfathers remember Isaac Johnson. I have reconstructed details of life along the St. Lawrence at the time Isaac Johnson lived and worked there. All of the places mentioned were important to him.

In 1994 a facsimile edition of *Slavery Days in Old Kentucky* was co-published by the Friends of Owen D. Young Library and The St. Lawrence County Historical Association. Copies of the book may be purchased by contacting the St. Lawrence County Historical Association, P.O. Box 8, Canton, New York 13617 (telephone 315-386-8133).

# I

# A New Home

THE RICKETY WAGON lumbered along in the dark over rough hilly roads. Around ten o'clock it rattled to a stop at a farmhouse on the banks of Beech Fork River. The farm was located about five miles south of Bardstown, Kentucky.

William Mattingly jumped to the ground. He nodded to his young slave to follow him. Isaac trembled as he peered into the darkness. He was seven years old, and no one had ever scared him as much as his new Master.

Sometimes his white father had fussed at him and his three brothers. But even though they were his slaves, he never threatened them. Isaac's black mother was not married to his father. At least not like white women were married to white men. She had been given to him to be his servant before Isaac was born. His father loved his mother. He never whipped her, or even treated her harshly like other slave masters treated their slaves.

"Peter!" Mr. Mattingly shouted.

A black boy emerged from the darkness. "Yes, sir, Master!"

"Have you put in feed for the horses?"

"Yes, sir, Master!"

Mr. Mattingly turned to the slave child he had purchased earlier in the day. "Come along with me!" he barked.

When they reached the house, Mrs. Mattingly opened the door. "What have you there, William?"

"I have a boy for you."

At the sight of the woman, Isaac yanked off his hat. He ran a hand through his black hair and straightened his shoulders.

"Indeed, you have a bright little fellow," she said.

"This is one of the Yeager niggers we saw advertised."

"I declare," said Margaret Mattingly. "He is not a very dark-colored one."

"No, wife, he isn't. He's one of those pumpkin-seed niggers from the mountains."

Mrs. Mattingly looked at Isaac. "I think he'll make a good servant," she said.

"I reckon he will when he gets that black snake around him a couple of times." Isaac cringed at the mention of the black snake. His eyes widened. His father had never whipped him nor his brothers.

"I don't think he'll need that. He doesn't look stupid like Peter."

Mr. Mattingly frowned. "I don't care if he is stupid. The black snake can correct stupidity."

Isaac had never heard such gruff talk at home. He stared at the floor.

"Stand up there! Let your Mistress look at you!" Mr. Mattingly commanded. "She hasn't half seen you yet."

Margaret Mattingly brought a lamp from the shelf. She studied the little boy. "What a nice little lad," she said. "And what a nice suit he's wearing!"

Mr. Mattingly snorted. "The idea of a nigger with a suit like that! Up on the mountains they don't know how to work the niggers! You just wait till I show him!"

"What's your name?" Mrs. Mattingly asked.

"Isaac," he answered without looking at her.

"That's a nice name." She paused. "You may take off your coat and sit down in the corner." She pointed toward the fireplace.

Isaac removed his coat and looked about for a place to hang it. Seeing none, he laid it on the little bundle he had brought with him. He crept over to the fireplace and sat on the floor.

Peter came in from finishing his chores. Mr. Mattingly quizzed him about the day's activities. Then he and his wife sat down to their supper of mush and milk. When they had eaten, Margaret brought a pan of the same food to Peter and Isaac.

"Peter," said his Master, after the boys had finished eating, "this little nigger is to help you in your work. He's green. You must teach him."

"Yes, sir, Master," said Peter.

Mistress Mattingly handed Isaac an old quilt. "This is for your bed," she said. "You and Peter may sleep together."

Peter already had a quilt. He stretched it out so that he and Isaac could lie on it in front of the fireplace. It did not take Peter long to turn in. He had nothing to take off. All he wore was a long tow shirt and a cloth cap. He pulled Isaac's quilt up under his chin, curled himself into a ball, and fell wearily to sleep.

Isaac sat in his corner thinking about home. His father never acted like Mr. Mattingly. He loved him. A tear crept down Isaac's cheek. He thought about his mother. Would he ever see her again? And what about his brothers? Why did the sheriff sell them in a slave auction? If his daddy had come home sooner, this wouldn't have happened. Something terrible must have kept him in New Orleans. Isaac shivered as he thought about his new Master, William Mattingly. So much had happened since the sheriff came to their cabin. Awful things were going on. He didn't understand them.

# 2

# The Farm on the Green River

IRISH SLAVE TRADERS had stolen Isaac's mother from her island home in Madagascar in 1840. They gave her to Griffin Yeager to be his servant. Mr. Yeager named her Jane. When he died a short time later, Jane was given to his eldest son, Richard. Richard "Dick" Yeager moved to a farm on the Green River in Kentucky. He took Jane with him and lived with her as though she were his wife. The farm was located near Elizabethtown, about a two days' journey from the slave market in Bardstown.

Dick and Jane lived together happily in their little cabin. The modest building had only two windows and one outside door. It was about twenty feet long and sixteen feet wide, and was divided into a kitchen and a bedroom. Jane cooked on the large flat stones in the kitchen fireplace, which also heated the cabin. When her housework was done, she helped Dick in the fields.

Dick built a little crib for their first son. They named him Louis. In 1844, a second son was born. They called him Isaac. A few years later Ambrose was born, and then Eddie, three years after that.

The first year they lived together Dick and Jane raised their own food, things like collard greens, snap beans, Irish potatoes, yams, and peas. They had enough to eat, but there was nothing extra.

The second year they tried raising hogs and tobacco. Every one of their hogs died, but the tobacco earned them cash—$1600. From then on they raised tobacco.

Each spring Dick and Jane worked together transplanting the tender tobacco plants. As soon as the boys were big enough, they helped by watering each plant once it was set out. They learned to pull the tobacco worms off the plants. In time the family became the leading tobacco growers in their area.

At first they had no neighbors nearer than ten miles. Eventually, neighbors moved closer to their farm. None of them were slave holders. They disapproved of Dick Yeager's manner of living. They didn't think he should live with a slave woman, or father her children. Though he was more prosperous than they were, they cut him off socially. They did not invite him to their gatherings. They refused to speak to him in public.

Dick Yeager did not like being ignored by his neighbors. He decided he would sell out. He would leave that part of Kentucky. He sold all his stock except his horses. He said good-bye to his family and took the horses to market in New Orleans.

Jane and the children waited for his return. He had been away for about two months when the sheriff came to the farm. The sheriff insisted he had orders to take the family to Bardstown. When they arrived there, he had them placed in the slave pen for the night.

Jane had never seen a slave pen, but she knew that was the place where slaves were confined when they were going to be sold at auction. Although she and her children were owned by Dick Yeager, he loved them and treated them well. She couldn't imagine why the sheriff had seized them and brought them to the slave auction in Bardstown. She gathered her frightened children about her as fears raged through her head. If only she could get a message to Dick. Something terrible must have happened to keep him away so long.

She needed to be brave for the boys. She could be sold to a different

Master than her children. She didn't know how she would bear that. She prayed they would be rescued before the dreadful auction began the next morning. If that didn't happen, she hoped she would be purchased by a Master as kind as Dick, one who would also buy her children. She couldn't imagine having a cruel Master. Her weary head drooped and she slept fitfully.

# 3

# The Slave Auction

THE SLAVE PEN was a frightful place. The slaves were crowded into stalls like animals. As the time for the auction neared, a crowd of jostling people would gather about the slave pen. A curtain kept the bidders from seeing the "stock" too soon. The overseer stood outside with a black snake whip and a pistol in his belt.

When it was time for the sale to begin, the curtains would be yanked back. The bidders would crowd around. Then the slaves would be forced out to a platform. They would be examined like horses. They'd have to hold their heads up, to walk briskly back and forth.

Buyers would feel their hands and arms and bodies. They would open their mouths and check their teeth. Sometimes they stripped them to the waist to see if they had scars. Scars on a slave's back showed that the slave was rebellious.

Mothers and small children were offered for sale together. However, if the bids were not high enough, they were sold separately. Jane thought of these things as she cradled her children in the slave pen that night.

The next morning a crowd gathered. The men took turns examining the slaves. Jane smoothed her skirt to make herself presentable after her restless night. At ten o'clock, nine-year-old Louis was led to the auction block.

"How much do I hear for this nigger?" The slaves cringed as the auctioneer asked for bids for Isaac's older brother. Louis was sold for eight hundred dollars. His mother cried out as her worst fears began to be realized.

The auctioneer called for Isaac. "Have you ever been whipped?" he demanded to know.

"No, sir," said Isaac.

He answered the other questions he was asked. Then the auctioneer shouted, "Time is precious, gentlemen. How much do I hear for this nigger?"

The first bid was four hundred dollars. Then five hundred dollars. Six hundred dollars. The bid was raised to seven hundred dollars by William Mattingly.

"Sold!" said the auctioneer.

William Mattingly came forward to claim his slave. "You come here, boy! Now you belong to me!"

"Let me go see my mother," Isaac pleaded.

"I'll train you without your mother's help," his new master muttered.

He grabbed Isaac and hitched him to a post as though he were a horse. Isaac remained chained to the post until late in the afternoon. He heard the auctioneer sell his little brother Ambrose to William Murphy for five hundred dollars.

Then his mother and his baby brother, Eddie, were placed on the auction block. At first there were no bids. Then someone called out, "Put them up separately."

"How much do I hear for the woman without the baby?" The first bid was for eight hundred dollars. In time Jane was sold for eleven hundred dollars. Finally two-year-old Eddie was sold for two hundred dollars to John Hunter.

Jane and each of her children had been sold to different Masters. They were not permitted to say good-bye to one another. Jane probably never saw any of her children again. Nor did Isaac ever see his brothers after that fateful day when they were sold at auction.

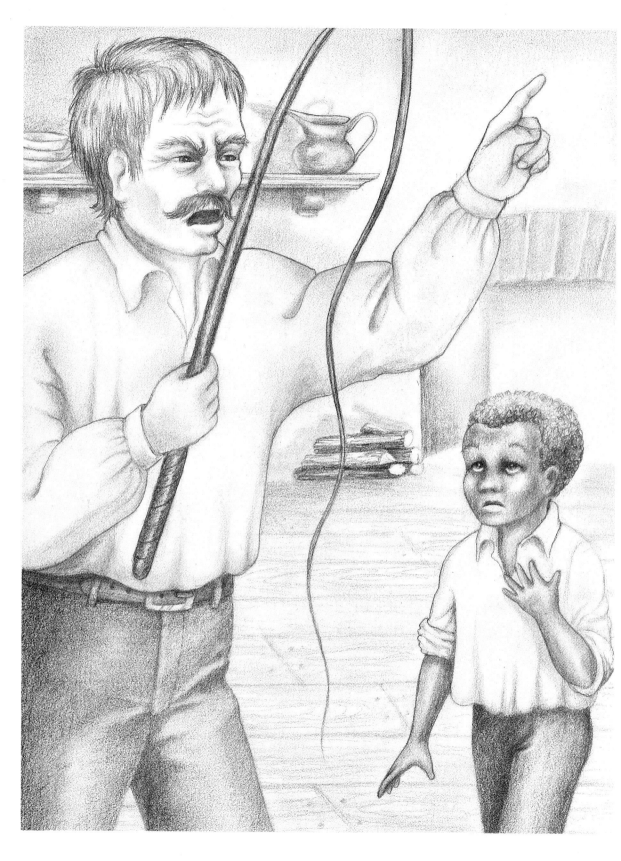

# 4.

# Master Mattingly

ISAAC MADE A PILLOW of his little bundle and lay down. But he couldn't go to sleep. He wondered what had happened to his father. Would he ever see him or the rest of his family again? The night wore on, but he did not get much rest. By and by he heard the voice of his Master calling.

"Peter! Peter! Are you awake?"

"Yes, sir, Master."

"Bring Isaac and show him what to do."

"Yes, sir, Master."

Peter showed Isaac where to get water while he split some wood for the Mistress. The boys finished their first chores of the day and went into the house for breakfast.

"Peter, have you done all the chores?"

"Yes, ma'am!" said Peter. He sat on the floor in one corner by the fireplace while Isaac sat in the other corner. Master and Mistress finished their breakfast. Then Mistress brought the boys mush and milk.

"Peter?"

"Yes, sir, Master."

"Go and hitch up the mules. Bring them ready to put on the grists for the mill."

The boys hitched up the mules and loaded them with sacks of corn. Master took Peter with him, but sent Isaac to the house. Mistress wanted him to help her with the washing.

When the washing was done, she asked him if he could iron. He said he would try. Mistress complimented him on his work. "You have done well, my boy. Now you may sit down and rest."

Isaac sat down and began to cry. "What's the matter, Isaac?" Mistress asked.

"I want to see my mamma."

"Don't cry. You'll see your mother again. Master will buy her and your brothers, too."

"Why didn't he buy them when he bought me?"

"Never mind about that. Your mother will be sold again soon and you will be together once more."

When Master and Peter returned to the house, William Mattingly asked, "Well, Margaret, how did you get along with the little nigger?"

"He's a good little worker," said Mrs. Mattingly.

"Have you taught him how to talk?"

"No," she replied, "but he'll learn without any trouble."

"That's the next thing he must learn," Master said. He turned toward Isaac. "Isaac, come here!"

"All right," Isaac answered.

"All right? Is that the way you answer your Master? When I tell you to come, you say, 'Yes, sir, Master.' I'll try you once more. Isaac, come here!"

Isaac was frightened. Again he answered, "All right."

His Master grabbed his whip. "Isaac, you nigger, you! If you talk to me that way again, I'll use this black snake on you! When I call you, you say, 'Yes, sir, Master.' Don't you ever say 'all right' to a white man! You do what I tell you or I'll try the black snake on your back! Now go and help Peter with his chores."

Isaac obeyed, but he didn't understand why he was treated so harshly. He helped Peter about the barn. They ate their supper, their second meal of the day, around 5:30 P.M. More mush and milk. Isaac was hungry. He was used to three meals a day. He wished he were back home with his family. They always had plenty of good food.

After supper he and Peter were sent to the corncrib to shell corn. They had to beat the ears with sticks shaped like hockey clubs. They worked until about ten o'clock. They shelled corn every night until the corncrib was empty.

When spring came, the boys helped with plowing, sowing, planting, and hoeing. New slave hands were brought to the farm every few days during the planting season. When the crop work was finished, the slaves would be set to clearing new land.

# 5

# Hired Out

WHEN HARVESTING was done and not so many slaves were needed for the farm work, many of them were hired out locally. This took place on the first day of January. In 1853, William Mattingly took some of his slaves to Bardstown. Their services for the year would be sold at auction. Isaac was hired out to a storekeeper named Yates for $100. Peter brought $125.

Isaac did chores at the Yates house and ran errands to the store about a mile away near Mammoth Cave. His hardest job was to carry water from the cave to the house. He wore a wooden yoke across his shoulders. At each end were hooks so that he could carry two pails at once. He had to enter the cave and descend about thirty feet to get the water.

Isaac heard people say that devils were living in the cave. They said the devils caught colored people and killed them. Isaac planned his trips to the cave when the sun was shining, so he could watch out for the devils.

Mr. Yates' sons were mischievous boys. After they discovered that Isaac believed the story about the devils, they went to the cave early each Sunday and built a fire. Then they sent Isaac for water. When he saw the fire, he was sure it was a devil, and ran home screaming.

The boys went back with him to the cave. By then the fire was out, and they accused Isaac of lying about seeing a devil.

Master Yates became suspicious of the devils who only appeared on Sundays. One Sunday he went with Isaac to get the water. He caught his sons building the fire. That ended the "appearance" of the devils in the cave.

Isaac remained with the Yates family until Christmas. He was given a week's holiday which he spent at William Mattingly's place. Then on January 1, 1854, he was sent to his Master's brother, James Mattingly.

James Mattingly owned two other slaves, a boy and a girl. He seldom left his room because he was usually drunk. He would order his slaves to his room and whip them for no reason.

One morning the boys were supposed to husk corn. It was raining, so they did not start at once for the crib. Master called them in to be punished. Isaac stood by as James Mattingly whipped the other boy. He knew his turn was next, so he ran home as fast as he could go. Margaret Mattingly saw him coming. When she asked him why he had returned, Isaac explained what had happened.

Mistress said, "Stay here till your Master comes home."

Isaac didn't know what his Master would say or do. But he was more afraid of James Mattingly, who was the meanest slaveholder he'd ever seen. When William Mattingly returned, he listened to Isaac's story.

"It's all right this time, Isaac. I've sold you to my brother, John. He lives on the Beech Fork River, about six miles from here. You can 'back' your things and I will take you there in the morning."

Isaac was relieved. "I've nothing to back," he said. "All I own is on my back. I can leave any time."

# 6.

## *Life on a "Stock Farm"*

EARLY THE NEXT MORNING William Mattingly took Isaac to his brother's farm. They rattled along for six miles. Isaac wondered how he would be treated by his new Master.

When they arrived at their destination, John Mattingly was away buying more slaves. His farm was a "stock" farm, the stock being Negro slaves. The location of his farm on the river made it easy for him to transport his purchases.

A few days after Isaac arrived at the farm, an attractive girl was sent there. Her name was Rosa. She was an octoroon (a person who is one-eighth Negro). The master had won her at a poker game in St. Louis. When he returned home, he kept her for his own use and made her stewardess of the stock farm.

John Mattingly owned one thousand acres of land, mostly covered with brush and bushes. He raised the usual farm crops. When the slaves were not needed in the fields, they cleared the land.

John had agents out in the country buying slaves and sending them to the farm. The year he bought Isaac, he had 120 slaves. After harvest, he sent the surplus Negroes to the Southern markets in Mississippi. The slaves were used to being sold from Master to Master,

but they dreaded being sold "downriver" to the Southern markets. That meant they would work even harder in the cotton fields.

The slaves never knew when they were to be sold. About ten o'clock the night before the sale, strong men stormed into their cabins. They handcuffed the men. In the morning they brought them out in pairs and fastened them to a chain forty to fifty feet long.

The line of march began. First, the chained men, next the women. Finally, the wagons packed with the children and the women unable to walk any distance. The destination was Nashville. There the slaves were placed aboard boats and taken downriver to the slave pens. The slave auctions were held from November until March.

In 1857, John Mattingly kept fifteen slaves to do the winter work. They husked and shelled the corn. They took it to the mill and then to the distillery to be made into liquor.

John Mattingly was about sixty when he married a girl only seventeen years old. He brought her to his farm along with twelve slaves. Rosa remained his stewardess, but the new bride became Mistress Mattingly.

New slaves were brought in every few days and set to work sixteen to eighteen hours each day clearing the land. The slaves were divided into gangs. Over each gang there was a boss who was also a slave. The bell rang at four o'clock each morning. Each boss had to see that his gang was up and ready for work. The gangs marched to the breakfast tables set up under some trees in the yard. A half hour later each boss marched his gang to the fields.

The overseer rode horseback from one gang to another to keep them busy. The slaves could not talk together in groups of three or more unless the overseer was present. If they disobeyed they were whipped.

At twelve o'clock the gangs marched to the dinner table. They had one hour to eat and rest. Then they marched back to work until sunset.

After their supper the slaves returned to their cabins. Ten to twelve persons lived in each cabin, though married slaves had their own cabins. Single men lived in separate cabins from single women.

At 10:00 P.M. the bell rang for bed. The overseer made his rounds at 10:30. Any slave not in bed was taken to the punishment cabin. In the morning he would be whipped by the Master.

# 7.

## A Time for Prayer

IN 1857, John Mattingly had about 200 slaves. In the fall most of them would be herded off to the slave markets in the South. The Master decided to take Rosa with him when he took his slaves to Bardstown to be sent on their way downriver. His young wife, a devout Catholic, was left at home to attend to the farm. While her husband was gone, she gathered the remaining slaves into her dining room. Each morning she taught them prayers. She taught some of the younger ones to read.

When the Master returned in the spring, he was angry at what she had done. He had told his slaves he was their Lord and Master. He lectured his Mistress.

"If you teach the slaves to pray and to read, they'll think they are human beings. We won't be able to keep them as slaves."

He scowled and went on. "The more ignorant we keep them, the better slaves they will be. The worst slaves we have are the ones who know the most. They're the ones we have to punish."

He paused for a breath. "We have 200 slaves each year. If they know as much as we do, what will happen to us? My dear, you must never again teach a Negro to read or to pray."

After the Master's lecture, there were no more gatherings for

prayer. The care of the slaves was turned over to Rosa. A few days later she took away their little prayer books and primers. "Master says you do not need them," she said.

The next Sunday John Mattingly seated the slaves on the ground in the yard and lectured them. "You must not think hard of me for telling you the truth about yourselves. The great God above has made you for the benefit of the white man. The white man is your lawmaker and lawgiver. Whenever you disobey His command, you must expect punishment."

He looked over his slaves to make sure everyone was listening. "You must never raise your hand against a white man. You are the same as the ox, the horse, or the mule. You were made for the use of the white man. You must do as he tells you. If you don't he will punish you just as he punishes the mule when he breaks him. That is the law that you must follow."

The Master dismissed his slaves and sauntered off to his house.

# 8

# A Friend for Isaac

BOB WAS ONE of the slaves brought to the stock farm that winter. He had been a free Negro in Canada. He had hired on the steamer *Louisville* at Cincinnati, Ohio, to work the round trip. When the steamer reached New Orleans, the cargo was sold. Just as the boat was ready to return to Cincinnati, the sheriff came aboard. He took all the Negroes who were not owned by a white man to the city jail.

For three months the sheriff advertised the Negroes as runaway slaves. Those who were not claimed were sold to the highest bidder. John Mattingly purchased Bob and took him to the next auction on his circuit. No one purchased him, so Mr. Mattingly brought him back to the stock farm. Bob was placed in the hoe gang over which Isaac was boss.

Bob was shrewd and strong, so he was watched closely. He was forbidden to talk to any of the men, but he was encouraged to associate with Rosa. In time he fell in love with her. The two talked freely.

Bob told Rosa about his home in Canada. "Why don't you run away with me?" he asked. "Black people are treated well in Canada. I can get us out of here."

He explained his plan for escaping. Rosa agreed to run away with him. They would flee when the heavy rains raised the Beech Fork River to flood stage.

Bob had also invited Isaac to run away to freedom in Canada. Isaac's part in the plan was to watch the river. He would let Bob know when the water was at its highest level.

The rains came and the waters rose. Isaac alerted Bob. "Now's our chance," he said. He had charge of the skiff and he knew how they could get safely over the dam in the river. It was Saturday. Isaac wanted to leave that evening.

"Not tonight," said Bob. "I want to take Rosa."

Isaac was horrified. "She'll tell Master. She tells him everything."

Bob refused to leave that evening or to go without Rosa. "We can go Monday morning," he explained. "Master is going away on Monday and will not return until night.

Isaac disapproved of taking Rosa, but he could not convince Bob that he shouldn't trust her. He had no choice but to wait.

Monday arrived. Master sent Isaac to get his horse. "I'm going to town," he said as he dismissed him to go to the field to work.

When he got to the field, Isaac informed Bob that Master had gone and the skiff was ready. He had left it at the "elbow" of the river.

"Take the boat around the elbow," said Bob. "Rosa and I will cross by land and meet you." Isaac headed off to follow Bob's plan. It was ten miles around the bend in the river, while across the land was only three miles.

The current was strong and Isaac reached the meeting place in good time. He waited for Bob and Rosa for nearly three hours. He decided he could wait no longer. He would set out on his own.

# 9.

# A Dash for Freedom

ISAAC MADE HIS WAY through the strong current. Bob had explained to him the whole route to Canada. He continued downstream till about seven o'clock in the evening. Three times men shot at him. The first shot hit the boat, but the other shots did not come near him. This encouraged Isaac.

"Fire away! You can't hit me!" he said. But he pulled harder until he reached the railroad bridge. He passed under it without being seen.

About a half mile inland Isaac saw a light. He assumed it was from a Negro cabin. He had not eaten since morning, and he was hungry. He pulled his boat ashore and started for the light. Before he had gone far, the light disappeared, so he headed back to his boat.

Two armed men with bloodhounds were searching the riverbanks. Isaac fled to the swamp. He stayed hidden for a couple of hours. Now he could see ten men looking for him. He knew he couldn't get away from them all. The longer he tried to escape, the worse it would be for him when he was caught. He knew what would happen if the dogs reached him before the men. So he gave himself up.

"I'll take him to my house," one of the slave catchers said. "I can return him to Mattingly in the morning."

Isaac was taken to the depot nearby where about fifty men armed with guns, knives, and dogs were gathered. They had all been pursuing him. Then Isaac was led to a house where he was given some supper and a place to lie down in the corner. His captor laid his revolver on the table. Then he went to bed with his wife in another corner of the room. The dogs slept nearby.

"I've got to get that revolver," thought Isaac. He would not go to sleep until he had found a way to steal it. But the day's events had tired him out. He had scarcely lain down before he fell asleep.

Next thing he knew he was being awakened. His captor gave him some breakfast. Then he was handed an axe. "You split this wood while I get the horses," the man said.

Isaac feared he had lost his last chance for freedom, but he didn't give up. As soon as the man entered the barn, Isaac tore out for the swamp. He had a quarter of a mile start before the dogs were set on his track. He reached the safety of the swamp and collapsed.

The bloodhounds passed on by, and Isaac headed for the river. He followed it until late in the afternoon. When he heard the dogs on one side of the river, he swam to the other. His skiff had disappeared, so he put together a raft.

He did not have time to push off. He heard the dogs nearby. Isaac plunged into the water and sank until only his nose and mouth were above the surface.

One of the bloodhounds picked up his scent. The dog yelped and started for Isaac. The hunters pointed their guns at him.

"Come ashore!" they commanded.

Isaac could not escape them. He swam ashore and surrendered. He was taken to the nearest depot. Shortly after he was returned to his Master, who paid fifty dollars to get him back.

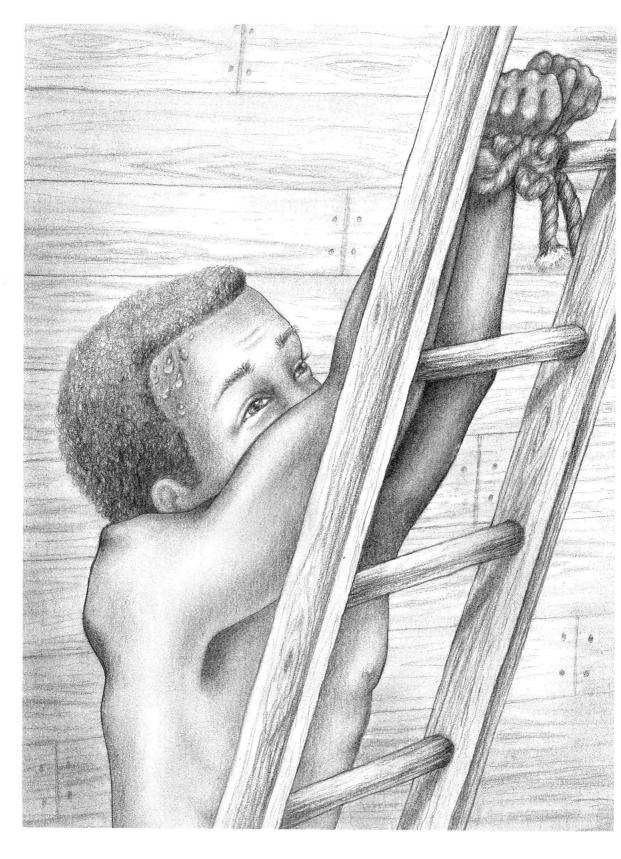

# 10.

# *Isaac's Punishment*

ABOUT A HALF HOUR after Isaac took off in the boat, Master returned home. When he discovered that Isaac was missing, he immediately sent for Bob. Rosa, perhaps out of fear, had betrayed Bob and told Master about his plans to run away to Canada.

As soon as Bob arrived, Master and three slave drivers pounced on him, lashed him with the black snake, and tortured him cruelly. They wanted him to die in agony. The other slaves would be forced to witness his suffering. John Mattingly would teach his slaves what happened to runaways.

Isaac was brought back to the Mattingly farm and taken to the garrett. Master handcuffed him to another slave to make sure he did not escape again. The next morning he was taken to the punishment room where he saw his friend, Bob, in misery.

When Master felt that Isaac had seen enough to keep him from trying to run away again, the slave drivers took him out into the yard. They stripped him of his clothing and strapped him to a ladder. Before they could lay the whip on him, the Master's wife spoke up.

"Let Isaac tell us why he was running away," she said.

"I wanted to go to Canada where I would be a free man," Isaac said.

"Who told you that you would be free in Canada?" his Master said.

Knowing that they couldn't hurt Bob any more than they had, Isaac answered, "Bob did."

"Who else knew about the plan to run away?"

"No one," said Isaac.

"Don't lie to me! Didn't Rosa know about it?"

Isaac replied, "If I thought she knew about it, I would not have run away. I knew she would tell you if she knew about our plans."

As the Master reached for his whip, the Mistress spoke again. "Isaac, I don't want to see you treated like Bob. If you will go into the garden and obey my orders, I will see that Master does not punish you. You must promise never to speak to a Negro on the farm. You may not leave the garden without my permission. You will come to my dining room for meals where Rosa will serve you. At night you must sleep in the garret."

She turned to her husband. "Let him go. I will look after him."

Isaac was led to the garden, which was surrounded by a high fence. The gate was locked and the key given to Rosa.

Bob suffered for five days. When he died, a funeral was held for him. All the slaves were brought in. Master preached a sermon.

"Bob was a bad man," he said. "I paid my money for him. I was his Master. If he had done right, he would not have died." He scowled at the slaves seated before him. "If you don't obey me, I'll whip you, too. I alone am your Master. When you do what I tell you to do, you will get along all right."

Isaac and the others bowed their heads in silence. Bob was safely out of reach of Master's cruel whip.

# II.

## The Civil War Begins

JOHN MATTINGLY'S STOCK FARM contained 120 Negroes in 1859. After the harvest season ended, he took most of them to the slave market. He purchased eighty more the next year. Once the crops were harvested, he took his slaves to market again.

But times were changing. Abraham Lincoln had been elected president, and in 1861 the War Between the States began. There was no market for slaves. John Mattingly had to return to his farm with the "stock." His slave trading activities were over.

The following year, the Union Army pushed its way into Kentucky and Tennessee. Whenever soldiers passed through their territory, the slaves hoped they would soon be freed. As Isaac watched the soldiers, he thought about Bob, and about freedom. If he could get to Canada, he would be a free man.

When Isaac heard there were troops encamped near his home, he headed out to find them. But he made a terrible mistake. The troops were Confederate soldiers from the South. They captured him and put him into their guardhouse, a large tent with a guard stationed in front.

Isaac's guardian angel was also on duty that night. A severe storm blew up and knocked down the guardhouse. In the confusion Isaac

melted into the shadows. He reached his home before anyone knew he had run away. He remained with John Mattingly for another year before making another break for freedom.

From the beginning of the war, great pressure had been put on President Lincoln to free the slaves. The President was opposed to slavery. Yet he did not want to interfere with slavery where it already existed. During the early months of the war, he fought to save the Union, not to free the slaves.

As the months went by, the Northern states demanded an end to slavery. By the summer of 1862, the President issued a preliminary proclamation. It said that the states that had left the Union must lay down their arms. They had to return to the Union by January 1, 1863. Otherwise, he would declare their slaves to be "forever free." True to his word, on January 1, 1863, President Lincoln issued the Emancipation Proclamation freeing the slaves.

The news that they were free was celebrated with shouts and songs and prayers by many of the Negroes. But some slaveholders did not tell their slaves they had been freed. Many years later, when Isaac wrote the story of his life as a slave, he did not mention the Emancipation Proclamation. Perhaps John Mattingly did not tell his slaves about it. While the war lasted, most of the slaves remained loyal to their masters.

Slavery was not abolished in some states until the 13th Amendment to the United States Constitution was passed on December 18, 1865. This new law freed all of the slaves in America.

The 10th Indiana Regiment had crossed the Ohio River and set up headquarters in Bardstown in the fall of 1861. Their encampment eventually moved to the William Sutherland farm "next door" to the Mattingly farm because it needed more space.

Isaac must have been aware of the large encampment on the neighboring farm. One day he heard there was a Michigan Regiment train coming through. He was at the mill the day he saw the troops. They had come within a mile of the Mattingly farm. He made a bargain with one of the men to go and cook for his captain. That night after he had finished his work at the mill, Isaac started out. When he overtook the troops, the guard halted him.

"I'm a friend," said Isaac.

"Advance, friend, and give the countersign," the guard replied.

Isaac advanced, but he did not know the countersign.

"What are you doing here at this hour of the night?" the guard demanded.

Isaac explained that he was hired by one of the men to cook for his captain. The guard accepted his explanation. He took Isaac to the man who had hired him.

Isaac turned in with the troops for the rest of the night. In the morning he was given breakfast and a new suit of soldier's clothing. He was driven to Lebanon to meet Captain Smith, Company A, of the 8th Michigan Regiment.

Captain Smith agreed to pay Isaac seven dollars a month to be his general servant. He hoped Isaac knew how to cook. He was willing to take his chances with the young black runaway.

# 12.

# *On the Trail of a Fugitive*

THE TROOPS CAMPED near the Mattingly farm for a couple of weeks. Then they moved on along the Green River. Isaac wrote to Rosa to tell her where he was. His letter fell into the hands of John Mattingly.

Mr. Mattingly headed for the encampment to claim his runaway slave. Isaac saw him coming while he was washing the captain's clothing in the brook. He hid until his Master went away. Then he took the clothing back to the tent.

Captain Smith asked, "Isaac, why are you so frightened?"

When Isaac did not respond, Captain Smith spoke again. "Something is bothering you. Did you see your Master?"

"Yes," said Isaac, "but he didn't see me."

"Well," said Captain Smith, "you can stop worrying about him. He went to the colonel and demanded your return. The colonel told him he hadn't come here to hunt runaway slaves. He gave him fifteen minutes to get outside his lines. Your Master left without asking any more questions."

Isaac sighed. Captain Smith handed him a revolver and twenty rounds of cartridges. "Take these to protect yourself." As Isaac reached out for them, the captain added, "If anyone demands your

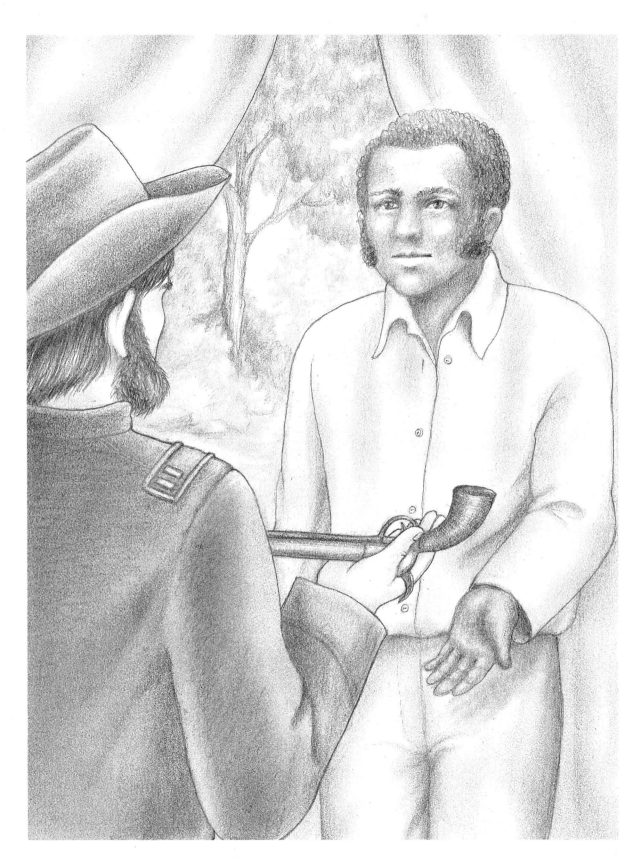

liberty, shoot him as you would a mad dog. If you don't, you deserve to be a slave."

As Isaac took the gun and cartridges, his shoulders straightened. For the first time in his life, he had been permitted to keep the money he earned. And now he had a weapon to defend himself.

After Captain Smith's term expired, he and many of his regiment re-enlisted. They were given a furlough. When they headed home to Detroit, they took Isaac with them.

In Detroit, Isaac looked across the river to Canada—the "Promised Land." It was the land of freedom that Bob had told him about. He was grateful for all Captain Smith had done for him, but Canada beckoned to him. He wanted to go there.

"I want to cross over into Canada," he told his captain. "I want to live where I'll really be free."

Captain Smith looked at him. "I understand," he said, "but I wish you'd return to the war with me."

Isaac considered his remarks. "I'd go with you if I could go as a soldier. I don't want to return merely as your servant," he said.

Captain Smith nodded. "The city of Detroit is getting up a colored regiment. If you want to fight for the freedom of your people, you should enlist with them."

Isaac was excited at the prospects of being a "real" soldier. He enlisted on February 3, 1864, with the 1st Michigan Colored Infantry. This new unit reached its full strength of 895 men by February 17 and became a part of the Union Army.

# 13.

# A Real *Soldier*

IT WAS SIX WEEKS before Isaac's regiment left Michigan. Those were difficult weeks. Blankets and clothing were scarce. Water dripped in through holes in the roof. It seeped in through the walls of their makeshift quarters. Some became ill. Others deserted.

Those who remained with the regiment were proud to be serving in the Union Army. When Isaac donned his uniform along with the other black soldiers, he expected to be treated with respect. The colonel of the regiment and black community leaders promised them the same privileges the white men enjoyed. But they did not get them. They often faced a hostile white community.

On March 28, 1864, the regiment left Detroit to join Union troops in Annapolis. Soon after, the regiment was renamed the 102nd United States Colored Regiment. The soldiers were dispatched to Hilton Head Island in South Carolina on April 16. They were commanded by a white officer, Colonel Henry L. Chipman.

This black regiment was praised for its military record, but its tour of duty lacked any real excitement. The men spent most of their time drilling and constructing fortifications. On August 11 they were attacked by a Confederate cavalry unit. After a brief skirmish, the enemy turned tail and fled.

Through the fall of 1864 the unit engaged in numerous skirmishes. Their severest test came at Honey Hill, South Carolina, on November 30. Three hundred officers and men of the 102nd joined Brigadier-General John Hatch's troops. Their charge was to break the Charlestown and Savannah Railroad. The artillery suffered severely from the enemy's fire. Many horses were killed. Two guns had to be abandoned. When darkness came, General Hatch withdrew his troops to Boyd's Neck.

Sixty-six Union soldiers were killed at Honey Hill, 645 others wounded. Isaac Johnson was seriously wounded in the right hand, losing his middle finger. Three bullets lodged in his left forearm. He was hospitalized at Beaufort, South Carolina, but the bullets were never removed. The bullets created some disability in that arm for the rest of his life. In later combat a shell fragment struck his heel.

The 102nd United States Colored Troops campaigned in South Carolina until the war ended with the surrender of Lee at Appomattox on April 9, 1865. Other Confederate troops soon gave up, too. The 102nd was assigned guard duty during the summer. Isaac Johnson was discharged from the Union Army on July 4, 1865.

# 14.

# *After the War*

AFTER HIS DISCHARGE from the Union Army, Isaac went home to Kentucky. He wanted to look for his family. He returned to Bardstown to the old Mattingly stock farm. Now that the war had brought an end to slavery, maybe he could find his mother and brothers.

When he reached the stock farm, he found John Mattingly paralyzed. He had not been out of his bed for six months. His former Master was suffering. Isaac was not sorry. He felt that Mattingly was being punished for torturing and murdering his friend, Bob.

John Mattingly appeared glad to see Isaac. "You were the first to leave me. Now you are the first to return," he told him. He offered him good wages if he would stay and work for him. But Isaac was not tempted to do that. He was twenty-one years old and a free man. He would not work for a man who had tortured his friend to death. He went in search of his family.

He found Rosa happily married to a colored man, who had been owned by a kind Master. He could not find his parents or brothers. From his father's brothers, Isaac learned the awful truth about the slave auction in Bardstown when he was seven years old.

His father, Dick Yeager, had arranged for the sale of his "wife" and children. He had sold his family for $3300. His brothers never

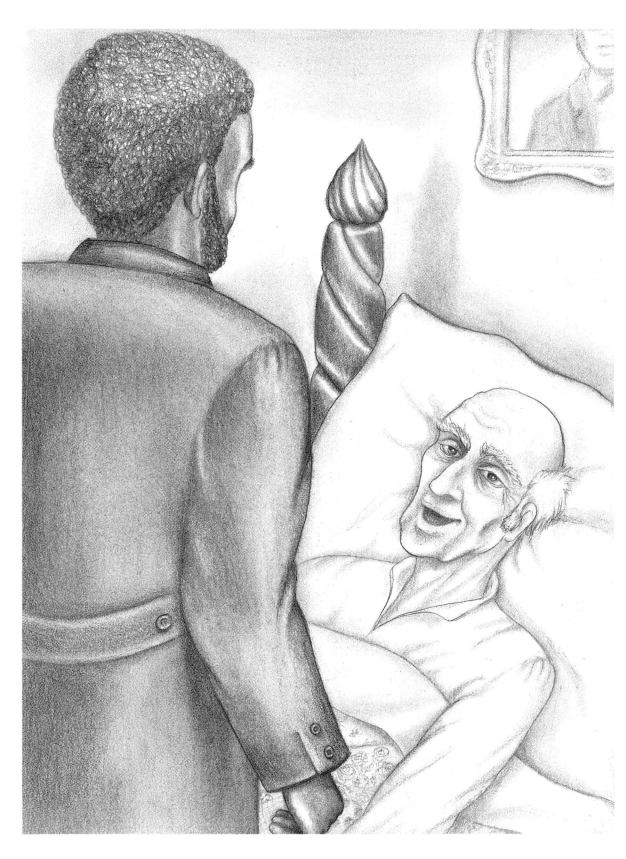

saw him after he returned to Bardstown to pick up his money. According to the town records, two years after he sold his black family, Dick Yeager married Mary E. Knott.

Isaac was stunned to learn that his father had sold his own family. When he thought about what slavery had made his master and his own father do, he preferred being in his black skin rather than in theirs. "Think of being obliged to associate with men of their stamp, say nothing about being their slave, and the mere thought is repulsive. A man who could sell his own children or who would uphold a system that enabled him to do so—the thought is a horror."

When Isaac learned the truth about the sale, he chose his mother's maiden name of Johnson as his own. He did not want to be known as Isaac Yeager.

# 15.

# Isaac in the "Promised Land"

ISAAC JOHNSON RECORDED his life as a slave in a book entitled *Slavery Days in Old Kentucky*. The book concludes with his visit to his old master and his learning that his father had betrayed his black family. The only records of Isaac's life immediately after the war are his military records from his service in the Union Army.

These records state that he was discharged in Washington, D.C., and that he lived in Louisville, Kentucky, until 1867. The Kentucky records do not list him. That is not surprising. Former slaves were fearful after the war. They did not draw attention to themselves, so many of them did not show up in the census.

When Isaac could not find any of his family, he moved north. According to the information he gave when he applied for a soldier's pension, he worked for a time as a sailor on the Great Lakes. Eventually he returned to Detroit. Then he crossed the Detroit River into Windsor, Ontario, in Canada. At last he had reached the "Promised Land" his friend Bob had described to him.

Isaac's travels brought him north to the St. Lawrence River port of Morrisburg, Ontario. Morrisburg was connected to Waddington, New York, by ferry and by other river craft. Isaac lived in the small villages along the St. Lawrence for the next ten years.

He drifted farther north to Winchester, Ontario, around 1870. The people of Winchester were mostly Scottish or Irish. Senior citizens in that area recall their grandfathers talking about Isaac Johnson. He is remembered as a handsome black man, about 5′ 8″ with wide sideburns reaching almost to the tip of his jaw.

Isaac Johnson lived in Winchester for seven or eight years. After moving about for a time, he settled into a log home across the road from the Baker quarry on the farm still owned and operated by the Baker family. The Bakers credit Isaac with developing the potential of the limestone quarry. They say he built the impressive stone house in which they live.

Isaac worked on several other private stone houses in the area. He employed a crew of stonecutters in the winter and masonry laborers during other seasons. Local residents identify two of the homes he built. One of them was for the Casselman family in Winchester Springs. The other home is located in Winchester.

Isaac Johnson was one of nine stonecutters who built the Winchester United Church. The church celebrated its centennial anniversary in 1983. John Benjamin Baker, church trustee and owner of the Baker quarry, had supplied the stone and lime for the building. He and his sons worked on the project for a year. Unfortunately, Mr. Baker injured himself lifting a large stone windowsill. He died before the building was completed.

A unique feature of this church is a sun, moon, and star on one of the outside walls. Why these designs were built into the church is a mystery. Some residents think they were signals to guide blacks who were migrating to Canada. Others feel the symbols might simply have been Isaac Johnson's "signature" as a stonemason.

Isaac was respected wherever he went. Stories and legends concerning him and his work are still shared among the descendants of those who knew him. One of the legends concerns his precise work. As the story goes, Isaac found that the north wall of the Winchester church building was out of line by half an inch. Although it had been raised to the tops of the windows, he tore the wall down and rebuilt it.

WINCHESTER UNITED CHURCH

Theadocia Johnson

From Winchester, Isaac moved to Morrisburg in Ontario where he lived for several years. About this time Morrisburg was at its peak of growth and prosperity. On December 28, 1874, Isaac married Theadocia Allen. He was thirty years old and well established as a stone-cutter and mason. Theadocia's parents, John and Louise Allen, were Canadian, but she was born in Chateaugay, New York.

The Johnsons' first child, Gertrude, was born in Winchester in 1876. Her sister, Susan, was born in 1881, also in Ontario. Through the years Isaac and Theadocia's family grew to nine. The other chil-

63

dren were twins named Louis and Louisa, Alice, Daniel, and Hattie. Three of the children were born in Waddington, New York. The Johnsons had moved across the St. Lawrence River to Waddington in 1884. Isaac continued his work as a contractor as well as a stonemason. It appears that he secured his own jobs with architects on both sides of the river.

THE CHILDREN OF ISAAC AND THEADOCIA JOHNSON

# 16.

# Stonecutter of the St. Lawrence

ALTHOUGH ISAAC JOHNSON spent his first years on the Green River in Kentucky and then was a slave of the Mattinglys on the banks of the Beech Fork River, the rivers did not influence his life. However, his life in Ontario and New York was vastly different.

Morrisburg and Waddington are both on the banks of the St. Lawrence River, and the river played a large part in the lives of everyone along its shores. Before the coming of the railroad to Morrisburg in 1855, the river and the canal system were the chief means of transportation. Riverside quarries provided stone for constructing buildings and bridges. It was an ideal place for Isaac Johnson to use his abilities as a master builder.

His skills as a stonecutter and stonemason were recognized by those who appreciated quality work. He was kept busy building houses, churches, bridges, and municipal buildings in both Ontario and New York. He was considered one of the finest stoneworkers. Just where and how he learned his trade is puzzling.

When Isaac was growing up near Bardstown, Kentucky, there were lots of stone fences built by slaves in Nelson County. But Isaac's skills were greater than the skills of stone-fence builders. His disability pension records list his occupation as farmer before he joined the

Union Army. So he must have learned to cut and set stone after the war.

It is possible that he learned his stonecraft after he migrated to Canada. There were lots of stonecutters in the Morrisburg area. Isaac, who seems to have been a quick learner, could have learned his trade from them.

When construction jobs were available in Waddington, Isaac moved his famiy across the river and continued his work as a contractor and builder. Two of the structures he built there are still standing: the Town Hall and the bridge at Chamberlain Corners.

## THE TOWN HALL AT WADDINGTON

The Town Hall in Waddington is one of the village's unusual structures. Its massive stone steps and heavy walls make it appear older

*Hope Irvin Marston*

WADDINGTON TOWN HALL

than it is. It was built in 1884 with Isaac Johnson as contractor. The building is 45 feet by 90 feet. It has an auditorium 20 feet high, and a tower 60 feet high. In the basement is a jail cell just large enough for one inmate—a testimony to the law-abiding residents of the town. An estimated 180 cords of stone were needed to build the Town Hall. (A cord is a stack that measures 4x4x8 feet.) The costs were set at $10,000, but later records give $15,500 as the final tally.

The hall, which has been placed on the National Historic Register, has been used as an opera house, dance hall, and basketball court. It's been a dining hall and a roller skating rink, a polling place, and a court of justice. It has also been used for religious services, graduation exercises, and for auctions. Church bazaars, rummage sales, and ice cream socials have been held there.

The hall was renovated about the time of its seventy-fifth anniversary. At that time the basement was converted to town and village offices. Through the efforts of the Town of Waddington, a grant was received for a second renovation, scheduled to be completed in 1995.

## THE BRIDGE AT CHAMBERLAIN CORNERS

When you travel from Waddington toward Norfolk, you cross the Grass River on an arched stone bridge at Chamberlain Corners. The original bridge was made of timber and planking. The sturdy stone one was built on solid bedrock by Isaac Johnson the same year he built the Town Hall in Waddington.

Local people say that the stone for the bridge was quarried from the riverbed or obtained nearby. The supporting piers of the bridge were built on bedrock. They were reinforced in 1930 by placing new arches under the old stone masonry. At the same time the roadway was widened to twenty feet.

Isaac built at least two more bridges in Waddington. These bridges were demolished when the St. Lawrence Seaway was constructed in

ARCHED STONE BRIDGE AT CHAMBERLAIN CORNERS

*Hope Irvin Marsh*

1958. The century-old bridge at Chamberlain Corners, with its five well-preserved arches, is still used as a main thoroughfare.

A story has been passed down concerning the original wooden bridge at Chamberlain Corners. A small circus was traveling from Norfolk to Waddington. An elephant was chosen to lead the caravan across the wooden bridge. The beast tested the structure with his front foot. Then he backed away. The circus wagons were driven over the bridge, but the elephant chose to ford the river. That elephant would not have been afraid to cross on Isaac Johnson's bridge. It could support a herd of elephants.

68

# 17.

# An Accident in Cornwall

WHEN THE IMMACULATE HEART OF MARY CHURCH at Churubusco, New York, was built, Isaac Johnson supervised the cutting of the huge stones. He laid the cornerstone for the church in 1888.

IMMACULATE HEART OF MARY CHURCH

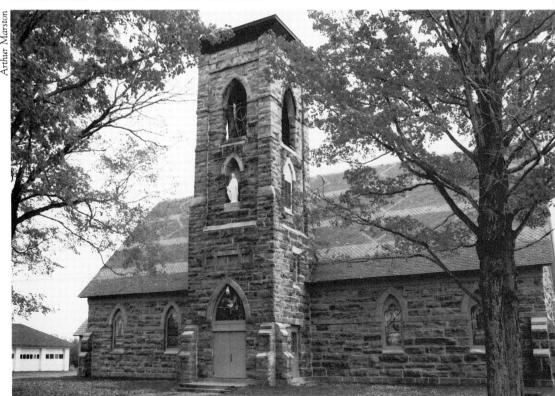

*Arthur Marston*

Isaac moved his family to the bustling port city of Ogdensburg, New York, when he did not find enough work in the Waddington area. The home in which the family lived still stands on Ford Street.

There were many jobs available for masons and builders in Ogdensburg because the state was building a huge asylum for the insane. A large number of administrative buildings and inmate cottages were built of stone or brick. The names of the builders are not recorded, but Isaac and his crews were no doubt part of the construction workers.

On November 1, 1897, while cutting stone in Cornwall, Ontario, Isaac fell from a derrick and fractured his right ankle. His gunshot wounds from the Civil War had limited his ability to work. This accident added to his disability, and a few weeks later he applied for a disability pension.

Now that his active working days had ended, Isaac had lots of time to think. And think he did—about his past and his children's future. He wanted to find a way to stretch his disability pension of only twelve dollars a month, so he could send his children to college. He decided to tell the story of his life as a slave. By telling the truth about slavery he would show the world what a horrible institution it was. And just maybe the sale of his little book would provide the funds needed to educate his children.

*Slavery Days in Old Kentucky* was printed privately in Ogdensburg, New York, in 1904. The forty-page booklet sold for twenty-five cents. Each of Isaac's children was given a hardbound copy of it.

Isaac's concern for the education of his children continues to bear fruit in the lives of his descendants. One of his grandsons, Jerome Eugene Nadine, earned a Bachelor of Philosophy degree and was ordained to the priesthood. He retired as a colonel in the U.S. Air Force in 1993. At the time of his retirement he celebrated his 35th anniversary as a priest. He presently serves in the Diocese of Reno/Las Vegas.

Isaac died at his home in Ogdensburg in 1905. He was sixty-one

JEROME E. NADINE, ISAAC JOHNSON'S GRANDSON

years old. According to his obituary in the local newspaper, he had suffered from heart disease for many months. He died suddenly at home while seated in his chair. He was buried in the Johnson family plot in the Ogdensburg cemetery. His wife, Theadocia, who died in 1908, and others of his family are also buried there.

THE JOHNSON HOME IN OGDENSBURG

# 18.

# *Isaac Johnson's Legacy*

ISAAC JOHNSON WAS SKILLED in carving wood as well as in cutting stone. When he lived in Winchester, he used to sit outside the hotel and whittle. A child's chair that he carved and painted is on exhibit at the John C. Moore Museum in Waddington.

The chair is coal black with an African-American motif. It was carved about 1873 for Katherine Scott, the five-year-old daughter of the hotel owners. After the chair was given to the museum by Katherine's daughter, Agnes Thompson, it became part of a traveling folk art exhibition called "Found in New York's North Country."

Isaac Johnson's churches and bridges and the Town Hall in Waddington stand as monuments to his skill as a builder and contractor. The bold way he escaped the bonds of slavery is a testimony to his character.

Many slaves crumbled under the terrors of cruel slaveholders and bloodthirsty slave catchers. Isaac's determination to be a free man enabled him to escape the hardships that slaves endured. He rose above the indignities, the hopelessness, and the frustration which his people suffered. His life story proves that one can overcome horrendous circumstances.

The first seven years of his life were lived as the happy son of a

CHAIR CARVED
BY ISAAC JOHNSON

Hope Irvin Marston

white father. In the preface to his autobiography, he says, "The hardships of my slave life were nothing in comparison with many." He wrote his story to give the world a knowledge of the evils of slavery, so that such a practice would never be possible again.

Isaac's book, *Slavery Days in Old Kentucky*, is an important part of his legacy. Few slaves were given the opportunity to learn to read and write. In some states it was forbidden by law to teach them to do that. Thus, it was unusual for a former slave to write a book, yet there were those who did write their life stories. They found a way to educate themselves.

When Isaac's story was written, he was recalling events that happened forty to fifty years earlier. But details were fresh in his mind. He never forgot the pain of learning that he and his family had been sold at auction at his father's request. Yet Isaac did not seek revenge against those who hurt him. He knew how to forgive.

On the final page of his book, Isaac Johnson wrote, "My people, for I call only the colored people mine, suffered for centuries, and

JOHNSON TOMBSTONE IN OGDENSBURG CEMETERY

the only wonder to me is that so many have survived, that they are so intelligent as they are, and as forgiving as they have shown themselves to be." And he concluded, "The manner in which they have used their freedom and treated their former masters appears to me they must have indelibly stamped in their natures the Lord's teachings, wherein He says: 'But I say unto you, love your enemies, bless them that curse you, do good to them that hate you, and pray for them which despitefully use you and persecute you, that you may be the children of your Father who is in heaven.' "

# Important Dates in Isaac Johnson's Life

1844    Isaac is born in Elizabethtown, KY. He is the son of Richard Yeager and Jane Johnson.

1851    Isaac's father sells him as a slave to William Mattingly for seven hundred dollars.

1854    Isaac is sold to John Mattingly to work on his "stock" farm.

1861    Isaac runs away to join the Union Army. He is hired by Captain Smith, who later takes him to Detroit.

1864    Isaac enlists in the First Michigan Colored Infantry on February 3.

1864    Isaac is wounded at Honey Hill, Deveaux Neck, and at Dingle's Mills.

1865    Isaac is discharged from the Union Army on July 4.

1867    Isaac moves north to Detroit and then to Morrisburg and Winchester, Ontario, Canada. He begins work as a mason and stonecutter.

1874    Isaac marries Theadocia Allen.

1884    Isaac moves his family to Waddington, NY, where he has contracts to build the Town Hall and the Chamberlain Corners Bridge.

1890    Isaac moves to Ogdensburg, NY.

1897    Isaac falls from a derrick at a stone quarry in Cornwall, Ontario.

1901    Isaac finishes writing *Slavery Days in Old Kentucky*.

1904    *Slavery Days in Old Kentucky* is published privately.

1905    Isaac dies of a heart attack at his home in Ogdensburg on December 5.

# For Further Reading

Adler, David. *A Picture Book of Harriet Tubman*. Holiday House, 1992

Altman, Susan. *Extraordinary Black Americans: From Colonial to Contemporary Times*. Childrens Press, 1989

Evitts, William J. *Captive Bodies, Free Spirits: The Story of Southern Slavery*. Julian Messner, 1985

Freedman, Florence. *Two Tickets to Freedom: The True Story of Ellen and William Craft, Fugitive Slaves*. Simon & Schuster, 1971

Hanson, Joyce. *Which Way Freedom?* Avon, 1992

Hanson, Joyce. *Out from This Place*. Avon, 1992

Johnson, Dolores. *Now Let Me Fly: The Story of a Slave Family*. Macmillan, 1993

Lyons, Mary E. *Letters from a Slave Girl: The Story of Harriet Jacobs*. Charles Scribner's Sons, 1992

Monjo, F. N. *Drinking Gourd*. HarperCollins, 1970

Ringold, Faith. *Aunt Harriet's Underground Railroad in the Sky*. Crown, 1992

Sabin, Francene. *Harriet Tubman*. Troll, 1984

Schulberg-Warner, Lucille. *From Slave to Abolitionist: The Life of William Wells Brown*. Dial Books, 1993

Stein, R. Conrad. *The Story of the Underground Railroad*. Childrens Press, 1981

Turner, Ann. *Nettie's Trip South*. Macmillan, 1987.

Turner, Glennette Tilley. *Take a Walk in Their Shoes*. Cobblehill Books, 1989

White, Anne Terry. *North to Liberty*. Garrard, 1972

Witner, Jeanette, *Follow the Drinking Gourd*. Knopf, 1988

# Index